Why We Are in Need of Tales

Part III

Why We Are in Need of Tales

Part III

discovering philosophical treasures in picture books

Maria daVenza Tillmanns

IGUANA

Publisher: Meghan Behse
Editor: Holly Warren
Front cover image: Diego Frayre
Back cover image: Abraham Roman

All drawings used with the permission of the artists and their parent(s).

ISBN 978-77180-566-7 (hardcover)
ISBN 978-77180-565-0 (paperback)
ISBN 978-77180-567-4 (ebook)

This is an original print edition of *Why We Are in Need of Tales, Part III.*

To those who have the courage to make hard choices

We Are in Need of Making Choices with Our Eyes Wide Open

A very, very long time ago, we all used to have tails, which would connect us to the world around us and to each other. Our tails also allowed us to communicate with each other with an incredible level of accuracy and nuance. With the slightest twitch of the tail, we could share our deepest thoughts and feelings.

But as time went on, we started to lose our tails. They became shorter and shorter until they disappeared altogether. And with their disappearance, we lost that mysterious connection to the world we live in and that mysterious connection to each other.

Huk and Tuk, the main characters in *Why We Are in Need of Tails*, discover that telling each other tales — or stories — helps us communicate our thoughts and feelings to better understand the world we live in.

And so, in *Why We Are in Need of Tales Part I and Part II*, Huk and Tuk share tales with each other and discover some of the philosophical treasures of life that are hidden within them. They discuss big questions like ...

How do I know whether something is truly mine or not?

What does it mean to belong to something?

What is so precious about friendship?

How do you explain something to someone who doesn't have the experience to understand your world?

How does willpower work?

When they discuss these tales with each other, Huk and Tuk exchange their ideas, their feelings, their questions. They don't always agree — and really, why should they? Huk is not Tuk and Tuk is not Huk. They are Huk *and* Tuk.

They learn that tales also transport us to realities outside of ourselves. I like to think of it as imagination travel. When we share tales, we share our imagination with fellow travelers. In that way, sharing tales is a lot like how sharing tails used to be.

One amazing thing about our imaginations is that our dreams — our dreams that connect us to the world we live in and to each other — become alive in them. Huk and Tuk discuss tales about dreams in Part II and learn about how it takes courage to follow those dreams by acting on them.

And in order to act on these dreams — or maybe you'd call them hopes or wishes for life — we have to make choices, and some choices are hard to make.

To make hard choices — any real choices! — we have to keep our eyes wide open. That way we can see what paths our choices might lead us down.

In discussing these next tales with each other, Huk and Tuk gain an understanding of the different choices we make in different situations — and how important choices can be. They decide that it's not always clear what the right choice is in every situation. There are lots of reasons we make certain choices, and sometimes we make mistakes too.

This little book is all about making choices and how complicated things can get when deciding what to do.

How Making Choices Can Make All the Difference

— Always by Arnold Lobel —

Huk and Tuk were out for a walk, gazing at the beautiful world around them — a world teeming with life.

See them? Huk pointed to some butterflies fluttering about.

Yes, Tuk replied, I do. Why?

Did you know those three butterflies do the same thing — the *exact* same thing — every day? Huk asked.

Why do they do the same thing every day? Tuk wanted to know.

They say they like it that way, Huk replied.

Don't they get bored? asked Tuk.

I don't think so, said Huk.

The story goes, Huk continued, that one day our friend Grasshopper, who is always on his way somewhere, got a bit tired of walking and decided to

by Anthony Ceron

sit down on a mushroom on the edge of the road. But right then, these three butterflies flew down and told him to move.

It turns out that these butterflies had a routine. All three would sit down on this mushroom together for a while *every day*.

But Grasshopper was sitting on that mushroom. Couldn't the butterflies go sit somewhere else? Tuk asked.

Apparently not, Huk said, because, as they told Grasshopper, they *always* sit on *this* mushroom at *this* time. So, Grasshopper — you know how Grasshopper is — decided to get up so the butterflies could sit there.

Once they were comfortably seated on their mushroom, the butterflies continued to tell Grasshopper that they do the exact same thing every day at the same time. *Always!*

Oh no! said Tuk.

Oh yes! said Huk, and they explained to Grasshopper that they like it that way. They wake up every morning, scratch their heads three times

— *always*. Open and close their wings four times — *always*. Fly in a circle six times — *always*. On and on — *always*. After lunch, they sit on the same sunflower and take the same nap — *always*. And they have the same dream about sitting on the sunflower taking a nap—

Okay, said Tuk before Huk could say *always* one more time. I get it. So how does this tale end?

Well, said Huk, the butterflies wanted Grasshopper to join their daily routine. They told him that they wanted to meet him every day and tell him about their scratching and flying while sitting on this mushroom they *always* sit on. And they decided that Grasshopper would listen to them the same way he listened to them that day.

But that's when Grasshopper decided that no, he wasn't going to do the same thing every day and that he would be moving on. Because he, Grasshopper told them, does something *different* every day — *always*.

I wonder, said Tuk, did the butterflies *decide* or *choose* to do the same thing every day, or did they simply *do* the same thing every day?

Good question, Tuk! We'll have to think about that one, said Huk.

Tuk didn't have to think very long.

Tuk's eyes lit up. Huk, Tuk said, you know the tale of Sisyphus, right?

I don't think so, Huk replied.

I'll tell you what I remember, Tuk continued. Sisyphus was the king of a big Greek city back when there were gods and goddesses of everything everywhere. He was cunning and managed to cheat death twice.

What! Huk exclaimed. How?

Once he cheated death by chaining up the guy in charge of death — that was Thanatos, Tuk added. But when he did that, no one died anymore. The second time, he persuaded Hades's wife, Persephone, who lives in the underworld — the world of death — to let him go back to his city. So, Zeus, the lightning bolt–throwing god of the universe, decided to punish King Sisyphus.

What was his punishment? Huk asked.

It can get pretty ugly, Huk thought, *when the gods decide to punish someone.*

Zeus made Sisyphus roll a boulder up a hill, Tuk replied.

Oh! Huk was relieved.

Then Huk asked, What's the big deal? Wasn't Sisyphus able to get the boulder up the hill?

The thing was, said Tuk, once Sisyphus got the boulder up the hill, it would roll back down again. And then he had to roll the boulder back up the hill.

And again and again and again and again, Tuk explained. Over and over for all eternity. That means *always*, forever.

That sounds awful, Huk said.

Tuk agreed. I learned about Sisyphus, Tuk admitted, by reading a book by a French philosopher. He wrote about the absurdity of life and said that we are always trying to find meaning in a meaningless existence.

Like rolling a boulder up a hill until the end of time, Huk concluded.

But then Huk looked confused. How can our *life* be meaningless?

Well, Tuk replied, Camus — that was the philosopher's name: Albert Camus — seemed to think we are all like Sisyphus in life, just rolling a boulder up a hill and watching it roll down again and going back to the bottom to push it up again and again and again. But he also said that if we can accept this fact, we can actually be happy. Imagine that!

Huk looked even more puzzled and confused. Can you be happy doing the same thing *always* like the butterflies, or pushing a boulder up a hill *always*? What is there to be happy about?

Well, Tuk mused, maybe, just maybe, if you *decide* — and you make it your *choice* — to push the boulder back up every time, or if you *decide* to sit on the same mushroom every day, it feels different. I mean, since you *decided* it, maybe that's what makes you feel happy.

If you just go along with things, you must feel so powerless, like you don't have a say in what's happening to you in your life at all, Huk said, continuing Tuk's thought. If you *decide* something, you have a say, a say in how you are going to act, even if nothing changes — even if you are going to sit on that same mushroom or push a boulder up a hill. It's your choice now and nobody else's. So yeah, that can make you feel good, or happy, I guess.

Do you think, Huk continued, Sisyphus ended up tricking Zeus again by being happy about his senseless plight, instead of being plain miserable like Zeus had hoped he'd be? Imagine, Huk said, could it be that Sisyphus outsmarted the gods a *third* time?

Yeah, Huk, you might be right, Tuk said, laughing.

Then Tuk continued, Do you think that what matters isn't whether you always do the same thing or always something different, but that you *decide* what you do?

Huk considered this for a minute while looking at the butterflies. Huh, Huk said. I think you might be on to something. It sounds like making our own decisions can be a pretty powerful thing. I never thought of it that way before.

How Making Choices Can Lead to Different Outcomes

— *Alone* by Arnold Lobel —

After their morning walk, Huk and Tuk headed back to Huk's house still laughing about those silly butterflies.

Tuk then felt inspired to tell a story. Here's a tale about Frog and Toad that you might know about, Tuk said.

As you know, Frog and Toad are the best of friends, and they do many things together, just like we do. They have adventures together too and share their experiences. And, what's more, they don't always have the same experiences of the same adventure.

What Tuk said made sense, too, because just like Huk is not Tuk and Tuk is not Huk, Frog is not Toad and Toad is not Frog; they're Frog *and* Toad.

Here's a tale, Tuk continued, where Frog and Toad have a totally different experience of what happened that one day. That day, Toad went over to Frog's house, and, to his utter surprise, he found a note on the door that said, *Dear Toad, I am not at home. I went out. I want to be alone.*

Toad couldn't believe it. Alone? he said. But Frog has me for a friend. Why does he want to be alone?

Huk, feeling somewhat anxious, interrupted Tuk's story, How would you feel if I left *you* a note like that?

I would be worried, too, Tuk admitted. Why would you want to be alone when you have me as a friend? Why would you suddenly decide to do something on your own?

Then Tuk remembered something. Hey, Huk, remember all those stories about dreams and imagination? All those individuals wanted to do things on their own, too, and their friends and family couldn't figure out why.

Yeah, said Huk. But why do we often think of someone going off on their own as something to worry about?

Well, Tuk replied slowly, maybe because, like the butterflies, we learn to expect certain things to stay the same, but then when one person — or butterfly or frog — chooses to do something different one day, we get worried, just like Toad did.

Everywhere Toad looked, Tuk continued — through the windows, in the garden, down Pebble Path — Frog was not there.

So, Toad went to the woods, the meadow and, finally, down to the river. Toad spotted Frog sitting by himself on a small island.

Toad did not think twice — maybe he should have — and decided that Frog must be very sad and that he should cheer him up.

He went home and put together a lunch with yummy sandwiches and a pitcher of cold iced tea. *That should make him feel better*, Toad thought. And Toad put everything in a basket.

When he got back to the river, he shouted: Frog, it's me, your best friend!

But Frog could not hear him. He was far too far away. Toad decided to take off his jacket. He waved it in the air, but it was no use.

What happened then? Huk asked.

by Diego Frayre

A turtle swam by, Tuk replied. So Toad decided to ask the turtle to bring him to the island where Frog was.

Frog wants to be alone, Toad told the turtle.

So why don't you leave him alone then? The turtle blurted out. Toad agreed and decided that maybe Frog wanted to be alone because he didn't want him as a friend anymore.

Toad got so carried away and cried out to Frog, I'm so sorry for all the dumb things I do and all the silly things I say. Will you *please* be my friend again? Then Toad fell off the turtle and into the river, basket and all.

Frog saw all the commotion and helped Toad onto the island. Toad explained that he had made the lunch to cheer Frog up but now the sandwiches were wet — yak! — and the pitcher was empty.

But I *am* happy, Frog said. I am happy because the sun was shining this morning and because I am a frog and because I have you as my best friend. I just wanted to be by myself and think about how wonderful everything is.

by Isaac Hernandez

Toad felt rather embarrassed and shyly said to Frog, I guess that's a very good reason to want to be alone.

Do you think he was convinced, Tuk? Huk asked.

I think so, said Tuk, but first he had to un-convince himself that Frog wanted nothing to do with him — to not even be his friend anymore.

Frog then told Toad that he was happy to not be alone now, and Frog and Toad ate the wet sandwiches and felt very happy being alone together.

How can they be alone and together? Huk asked.

Well, said Tuk, I think it's like when you and I sit quietly together gazing at the world around us. We're alone *and* we're together.

But why do we think something is wrong when someone chooses to do something on their own? Huk wanted to know.

Maybe Toad thought something was wrong because Frog did not include him in his decision to want to be alone. I mean, Tuk said, if Frog had decided to tell Toad — not just left him a note — Toad might not have been so worried.

Perhaps, Huk said. But do you know what else I think? I think Frog must feel really good that he has a friend like Toad who wanted to make sure his best friend was happy and brought him a delicious lunch — before it all fell into the river, I mean.

Tuk agreed, Toad is a really good friend. Then Tuk laughed and added, When they were alone together, they reconnected their tails. I know frogs and toads don't have tails, but you know what I mean.

I do, responded Huk.

How We Sometimes Choose to Change Our Minds

— The Missing Piece by Shel Silverstein —

Both Huk and Tuk felt hungry after the tale about Frog and Toad, so they started to prepare lunch together.

They made toasted sandwiches of thinly sliced hard-boiled eggs with salt and pepper, and some cherry tomatoes on the side. For dessert, they had some delicious fresh figs.

Tuk was still reflecting on the tale about Frog and Toad. I think, Tuk said, that Toad was afraid something was missing in their friendship and, suddenly feeling alone, got really worried. But in the end, nothing was missing, and he realized he was not at all alone.

Yeah, Huk said, sometimes we can feel like something's missing when it isn't. It can happen in relationships, but it can also happen in ourselves. It can feel like we're not whole, you know?

I heard a tale about a something who felt like they were missing a piece and went on a quest to find it.

Did they find it? Tuk asked while munching on some of the cherry tomatoes.

Well, guess what? Huk continued, On their journey, they actually found out they were not missing anything.

Huh? Tuk said, confused about where Huk was going with this.

Let me explain, said Huk. This something looked like a circle with a piece cut out of it, kind of like a pie missing a slice.

Oh yum, pie! Tuk said.

Huk looked over at Tuk's smiling face, then continued telling the story. Anyway, Huk said, let's call the pie-like something Sandy. In the tale, she doesn't have a name, but I think it'll be easier for me to tell the tale if we give her a name.

So, Sandy decided to go looking for her missing piece. She rolled along looking for it, and she sang a missing-piece song.

On her way, she got hot in the sun and wet in the rain and cold in the snow. Because of her missing piece, she could not roll very fast, so she had time to talk to a worm, to smell a flower and to watch a beetle as she rolled past. She went over oceans and through swamps and up and down mountains, until one day, when she stopped because she thought she had found her missing piece.

But the piece called out to her and said he was not her missing piece, because he was nobody's piece. He was his own piece.

Sandy felt a bit foolish. She apologized and rolled on.

As she rolled, she kept finding all kinds of pieces, but they were all too small or too big, too this or too that. But she didn't give up. Sandy continued on. She had all kinds of adventures on her journey — she fell into holes, and she bumped into walls.

Finally, Sandy *did* find a piece that seemed to fit. And she tried it on, and it *did* fit. It fit perfectly — at last.

That's great, said Tuk. Sandy could go home feeling whole now.

You might think so, said Huk, but actually, the interesting part comes next, because now that Sandy

by Isaac Hernandez

had her missing piece, she ended up rolling faster and faster than ever before. Too fast, in fact. And because she was rolling so very fast, she could not talk to a worm or smell a flower or watch a beetle. And when she wanted to sing her missing-piece song, she could not utter the words right. They got all garbled up.

She became terribly unhappy. Sandy then opened her eyes wide and changed her mind. She decided to go through life without her missing piece and to go back to the way things were. She put the missing piece down and rolled away, singing her missing-piece song as before. Along her journey, she rolled slowly enough to talk to a worm and smell a flower and enjoy watching a beetle as before. And she felt so happy.

Wow, Tuk said. I'm surprised Sandy would decide to give up the piece she spent all that time looking for.

I think Sandy might have actually felt more whole without the missing piece, Huk replied.

Do you think the story is saying you're more complete when you're not complete? Tuk asked.

That sounds very philosophical, Huk said, laughing. But I think that might be it. Sandy was more complete when she rolled slowly so she could talk to the worm and smell the flower, watch the beetle and sing her song. She felt more whole without her missing piece because she felt *connected* to everything around her again, as she did when she set out on her journey to find her missing piece.

So, she was whole all along but didn't realize it? Tuk asked. I guess this adventure opened her eyes and made her realize that it is much more gratifying to move slowly and to feel connected to the world of worms and flowers and beetles around you than to rush by quickly on your own.

How Certain Choices Can Hurt Others

— *The Giving Tree* by Shel Silverstein —

Huk and Tuk contemplated how being incomplete made you more complete or whole — as in the pie-like something's case — because it gave you the chance to connect to the world around you.

Sandy realized that being complete made it harder to live the way she wanted to, Tuk said. And that tale had a happy ending, but I know a sad tale about how the feeling of missing something never ends and looking for more and more "missing pieces" never made the boy in the tale happy.

Will you tell it to me? Huk asked.

The thing is, Huk, the tale starts off really nice and warm, Tuk said, but then it becomes colder and colder. Do you think you still want me to tell it?

How about we sit by the fireplace to comfort ourselves while you tell this sad, cold tale? Huk suggested. The warmth of the fire should help.

They huddled close to the fire.

Once upon a time, Tuk began, there was a tree and there was a little boy.

The little boy loved visiting the tree often. He would make a crown out of her leaves and pretend he was a king. He would climb up her trunk, swing from her branches and eat her apples.

The tree loved the boy. The boy loved the tree. The tree was happy. The boy was happy.

As the boy grew older, he stopped coming to visit every day. And the tree was often alone.

After a long while, the boy returned, and the tree invited him to climb up her trunk, eat her apples and be happy like before. But this time the boy, older now, said he was too old to climb and play.

Instead, the boy asked the tree, can you give me money?

I can't, the tree replied, but you can take my apples and sell them in the city so that you'll have money and be happy.

And the boy did just that. He shook all the apples

by Diego Frayre

out of the tree and carried them away. The tree was happy she could help.

Was the boy happy? Huk asked.

I don't know, Tuk said. Maybe ... but I don't think they were happy *together* as they used to be, like Frog and Toad are or like we are. Their relationship changed and it wasn't what it was before.

After the boy took all the apples, Tuk continued, he didn't come back to visit for a very long time.

And the tree was alone for a very long time, Huk interjected.

That's right, Tuk said, so when the boy returned, the tree shook with joy! It had been such a long time since she had last seen him. She invited him again to climb up her trunk and swing from her branches. But the boy only said that he was too busy now. He wanted a house to keep him warm. He wanted a family.

Can you give me a house? he asked her.

No, she replied, but you may cut off my branches and build a house. Then you will be happy.

So, Tuk continued, the boy cut off all her branches so he could build his house. The tree was happy.

by Roger Gutierrez

What! Huk interrupted. Do you *really* think the tree was happy? Helping the *boy* out made her happy, but what I mean is, was *she* happy?

The boy never did anything to make *her* happy, that's clear, Tuk replied. When he was a boy, he came every day to see her and be with her. But when he grew up, he just visited her when he wanted things. The relationship was taking a turn for the worse, if you ask me, Tuk said, because the boy was no longer connected to the tree — he just wanted things from her.

I don't like the boy, Huk blurted out. He's taking the tree for granted. He could have visited her with his family and his kids, who could climb up her trunk and swing from her branches.

I don't like the boy either, Tuk said. He doesn't seem to appreciate all she's doing to make him happy.

I wonder why the tree loves the boy so much, Huk said.

That's hard to say, Tuk said. Maybe it's important for the tree to see the boy happy no matter what.

So how does this sad tale end? Huk asked.

Well, said Tuk, the next time the boy left, he stayed away for even longer than ever before. By the time he did show up, he was old and tired. He asked the tree for a boat to sail away with.

Did she give him the boat? Huk asked.

Of course, Tuk said, in a way. The tree let the boy — or, I guess he was a man now — cut down her trunk so he could make a boat and sail away.

Huk moved closer to the fire and said, That's so sad. The boy sounds like he's looking for all sorts of things — all sorts of missing pieces — to make him happy. But he's never really happy, ever.

Why do you think he kept coming back? Huk asked.

I don't really know, Tuk said. Maybe because he knew she loved him and that she would do anything to make him happy. She seemed happy every time she gave him something of her tree.

I think he's a sourpuss, Huk decided. He's never really happy or grateful.

In the end, Tuk said, the boy came back one more time. And when he returned, the tree told him she had nothing left to give.

by Brettany Villalobos

I'm just an old stump, she said. And the boy replied, I don't need very much now, maybe just a quiet place to sit and rest.

Well then, the tree said, come sit and rest. Stumps are good for sitting on and resting. And the boy did. And the tree was happy.

But the tree is dead now! Huk cried out. She can't grow back a trunk and branches and apples...

Yes, the tree is dead now, said Tuk. That's why it's a very sad story, I think. And it's a tale about how the boy took the tree and her love for him for granted.

The fire in Huk's fireplace was slowly going out, and Huk and Tuk were feeling very sad together.

Then Tuk said, It's like when we just take the world for granted and use up everything the Earth gives us and think little of it because we figure that's what the Earth is for. Just like the boy thought the tree was there to give him want he wanted and needed. It's about time we opened our eyes wide and made some real choices about how we treat the world instead.

When we all still had tails that connected us, Huk said, nobody acted the way that boy did. We felt connected to everything and we made decisions with our eyes wide open about how to treat the Earth, because we realized our choices affected others too.

And the tree can't give anymore when she's dead, Huk said, no matter how much she loves the boy.

I know, said Tuk, that's why this is such a sad tale.

How Making Choices Can Inspire Others

— Tico and the Golden Wings by Leo Lionni —

Tuk stayed over at Huk's house that night. Thankfully, by the time they got up in the morning, the sun was shining, and they both felt happy again.

Every day *is* a new day.

At breakfast, they sat sipping their hot tea and eating their berries and fruits and cinnamon toast.

Tuk looked thoughtful and then said, Huk, I know another tale about giving. It's about a bird named Tico who gives all his golden feathers away. This tale has a good ending.

Oh great, said Huk, we could use some cheering up.

In the tale, Tico starts by telling us about himself, Tuk said. He's not sure how it happened, but he says he was born with no wings. He sang and hopped around like the other birds, but he couldn't fly. Luckily, his friends loved him and brought him berries and fruits and took good care of him.

But Tico was sad that he could not fly. He would ask, Why can't I soar through the sky like the others? And he would wish for golden wings so he could fly high over the mountaintops.

Then one night, Tuk continued, Tico was awakened by a peculiar sound. He opened his eyes and saw a wishing bird. The wishing bird told him to make a wish and promised that it would come true.

Tico told the wishing bird about his dream of having golden wings. Then a flash of light appeared, and the wishing bird vanished in the deep dark sky.

His wish had come true: Tico had a pair of golden wings.

Tico wasn't sure if this could be real, so he opened his wings slowly and cautiously started to fly. When he felt the wind beneath his wings, Tico flew over flower patches and saw a river below that looked like a silver necklace. Oh, the world was mesmerizing!

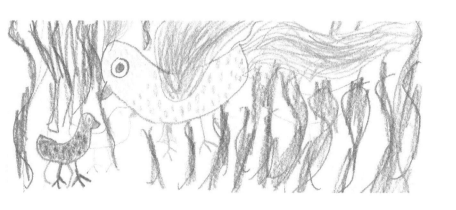

by Kairi Pacheco

by Kaelie Lopez

But when he flew back to be with his friends, they said things like, Now you think you're better than us with your golden wings?

And they jeered at him, You always wanted to be different.

Then they all flew away.

After his friends left, Tuk continued, Tico started to feel very lonely. Although he had beautiful golden wings and could fly like his friends now, they had all left him.

Huk said thoughtfully, Life is hard without friends.

But were they really his friends? Tuk wondered. Would friends just fly away and leave you all by yourself like that?

They also accused Tico of wanting to be different, Huk said.

But he was also different from them when he had *no* wings, Tuk said, and they cared for him then. They took care of him by bringing him fruits and berries.

So, what changed? Huk wanted to know. Were they jealous now that he had golden wings?

For a minute, Huk was lost in thought.

Then Huk looked at Tuk and said, You know, being different can be a good thing or a bad thing, just like being alone can be a good thing or a bad thing. And being complete can mean being incomplete sometimes. Things seem to always be kind of complicated that way.

Tuk agreed that life is a lot more complicated but didn't know what to say because it is so complicated.

Tuk continued with the tale instead. While Tico sat all alone and felt miserable, his eyes suddenly opened wide, and he spotted a basket maker who had many baskets lying all around him. Tico noticed that the basket maker was crying.

Why are you sad? Tico asked the basket maker. The basket maker told him that his child was very sick, and he didn't have the money to buy the medicine his child needed. He was too poor.

Then Tico thought about how he could help. He decided to give the basket maker one of his golden feathers.

The basket maker was grateful and thanked Tico for saving his child's life.

That's so sweet, Huk said. Tico must have felt happy knowing that he'd helped the basket maker and his child.

He did, Tuk said. But look, suddenly something else happened. There was now a beautiful silk black feather where the golden feather had been.

Tico started giving his golden feathers to people who needed help. He gave new puppets to a poor puppeteer, a spinning wheel to help an old woman make a shawl and a compass to help guide a lost fisherman. After Tico had given away his last golden feather, his wings were as black as India ink.

At least Tico still had wings to fly, Huk said. I like that about this story. It's not like the tale about the giving tree who gave and gave until she had nothing left.

I know another way it's not like that tale, said Tuk. The tree gave everything to a boy who only wanted more, but Tico gave to people who really needed — not just *wanted* — the things Tico gave.

Exactly! said Huk. And another really important way it's different is that those people Tico helped

by Abraham Roman

out were all so happy and so grateful, not like that sourpuss boy.

Did Tico go back to his friends? Huk wanted to know.

Yes, Tuk said, he wanted to be with his friends again, but he was worried they might not welcome him back. But they were all happy when they saw him and said, Now you are just like us.

Tico and his friends huddled together, and Tico was so happy, he couldn't sleep. He happily thought of all the things he had done while he was away from his friends and realized that even though his feathers were black like his friends' feathers, he wasn't just like his friends. He'd had lots of different experiences they did not have.

That's true, Huk said, then added, Tico was different now in another way, too. His sort-of friends had no idea what he had done with his golden feathers. They simply liked that he now looked just like them.

I think, Tuk concluded, that when Tico's eyes were wide open, he connected to the world around him and to the people he saw who needed help. He was able to see that they were in need, and that's when he decided to help them.

It seems that his friends had their eyes half closed, Tuk added, since they only saw that Tico now looked like them with his black wings. And it seems that's all that mattered to them.

But you forget, Huk said, they did help him when he didn't have any wings at all, remember?

True, Tuk admitted, but when he had golden wings, they figured he felt like he was better than them, and they just flew off, leaving him alone. I mean, they didn't see Tico as a threat when he had no wings, is my point.

Well, Huk concluded, I guess they reconnected in some way. His friends were happy he looked like them and Tico was happy to not be alone.

How Making Hard Choices Is Never Easy

— *Doctor De Soto* by William Steig —

After Huk and Tuk finished their breakfast, they decided to go out for a stroll. They walked through the meadow covered in wildflowers and along the creek with tall grass rising from its banks. While they walked, they could hear birds chirping in the woods nearby. It was a peaceful morning, and the air was fresh and cool.

As they approached Tuk's home, they passed the crumbling wall where a mouse family lived.

You know, said Huk, as a mouse scurried by, I know a tale about a mouse dentist. Isn't that funny?

The mouse was named Doctor De Soto, said Huk. He was the only dentist — I think — in his small town, and his wife, Mrs. De Soto, was his assistant. Doctor De Soto had been the town dentist for many years. He helped the large animals as well as the smaller animals, but he refused to help animals that were dangerous to mice. The shingle outside his office said as much. It read:

Cats and Other Dangerous Animals
Not Accepted for Treatment

One day, as the De Sotos took a break and looked out the window, they saw a well-dressed fox with a bandana tied around his jaw.

Doctor De Soto quickly assessed the situation and called out the window, I cannot treat you, sir. Haven't you read my sign?

But the fox wept so bitterly and seemed to be in so much pain. Please, he wailed, have mercy. I am suffering.

Doctor De Soto and his wife were troubled. Should they let him in or not? A fox is dangerous to mice. That was obvious. But the fox was in terrible pain. That too was obvious.

Would you let him in if you were the De Sotos? Tuk interrupted Huk's telling of the tale. I mean, you would want to help someone who's in terrible pain, but what if your life were on the line? That's serious.

That seems like an impossible decision to have to make.

I don't know, said Huk. How do you even begin to decide something like that?

I'm not sure, said Tuk. Doctor De Soto's job was to help those who need help and so it makes sense that he would want to honor his commitment to helping others.

I know, Huk replied, but I think he also didn't want to end up like the giving tree — dead! And that's why his sign says specifically that he won't help those dangerous to him and his wife.

Even though he's the only dentist in town who can help those in need? Tuk continued. That's a really hard decision to make, you know.

So, what does the story say? Tuk asked, hoping to avoid the question altogether.

Well, as the story goes, Huk said, Mrs. De Soto *did* know what to do. She decided they should risk it. She pushed the buzzer to let the fox in.

The fox was up the stairs in no time. He fell to his knees and cried, My tooth is killing me. Please, please do something. I beg you.

Doctor De Soto went straight to work. Please remove the bandana, sir, he said, and have a seat on the floor over here.

Remember, Doctor De Soto is a mouse, Huk continued, so he needed to climb up a ladder to reach the fox's mouth. Open wide, he said, and he climbed into the fox's mouth, which was not at all a comfortable place for any mouse to be.

Doctor De Soto discovered the problem immediately. The fox had a thoroughly rotten molar and terribly bad breath. He told the fox that the tooth would have to come out. But he promised to make the fox a new tooth to replace it.

The fox agreed. Just make the pain go away, he wailed. But a fox is still a fox, and he could not help thinking how delicious the De Sotos would be to eat. The thought alone made his jaw quiver.

Keep open! Doctor De Soto yelled.

I think Doctor De Soto is terribly brave, Tuk said. I don't think I would have had the nerve to do what that mouse did. Imagine! Entering the fox's mouth? That's unbelievable!

by Kairi Pacheco

I know, said Huk, just telling the tale makes me nervous. So then, Huk continued, Doctor De Soto, with the help of his wife, gave the fox some gas so he would not feel anything when they yanked the tooth out.

Soon the fox was in dreamland. And in his dream, he mumbled, Mmm, yummy, raw with a pinch of salt, and a dry white wine indeed!

It was clear what he was dreaming about. The De Sotos quickly placed a pole in the fox's mouth to make sure it stayed wide open. Then they fastened the extractor to the bad tooth and turned the winch. And the rotten molar came out!

When the fox came to, Doctor De Soto told him to return the next day so he could put the new tooth in its place. Be here at eleven sharp, he told the fox.

Still somewhat dizzy from the gas, the fox went back home. But on the way, he couldn't help thinking — after all, he is a fox — whether it would be in bad taste (no pun intended, Huk said and giggled) to eat the De Sotos after the job was done.

Back at the dentist's office, Doctor De Soto muttered, Raw with salt indeed! How foolish we were to trust a fox. It's like we didn't even read our own sign out front stating *clearly* that animals dangerous to mice would not be accepted for treatment.

Mrs. De Soto, on the other hand, thought the fox would not harm them. After all, they were helping him.

You don't understand, Doctor De Soto said, a fox is a fox. What do you expect? He doesn't choose to be a fox. A fox is a fox is a fox and that's that. He can't choose not to be one.

That night they lay in bed worrying and wondering whether they should let the fox in the next day. They had already helped the fox by pulling his rotten tooth. Should they do more than that?

Would you let the fox in a second time? Tuk asked Huk.

Ha! Huk exclaimed, now thoroughly convinced. I would not even have allowed him in in the first place. And you?

Tuk didn't want to appear as scared as Huk seemed to be, and nonchalantly said, Well, I'd have to think about that.

So, Huk continued, Doctor De Soto made it clear that once he started a job, he always finished it. He was determined to let the fox back in the next day at eleven o'clock sharp.

A very cheerful fox showed up the next morning.

The fox was thrilled. The gold tooth was beautiful. Doctor De Soto set it in the socket and hooked it up to the teeth on both sides.

The fox figured he really shouldn't eat the De Sotos, but how could he resist? Did he have a choice in the matter? That was the question.

Then, before letting the fox go, Doctor De Soto explained that they were not quite finished and that he and his wife had recently developed a remarkable ointment that would prevent any toothaches in the future.

The De Sotos expected the news to sound like music to the fox's big ears. And it did! The fox was delighted and was eager to try the ointment.

In the meantime, the fox had made up his mind to eat the De Sotos with the help of his brand-new tooth.

Why are foxes so mean? Tuk asked. The De Sotos helped him. Isn't that something for the fox to consider, Tuk asked, and at least *try* to resist eating them?

Are foxes mean? Huk responded. Or is it simply their nature to eat mice?

Mean or not mean, it's just not right. So then what? Tuk wanted to know, worried that the fox was going to eat the De Sotos.

So, Doctor De Soto carefully applied the ointment on all the fox's teeth.

The fox looked extremely happy. He was enjoying the best of all worlds — no more pain, an ointment that would prevent toothaches forever and, last but not least, a delicious delicacy before leaving the dentist's office.

Then Doctor De Soto told the fox to close his jaws tight and to keep them closed for a minute so the ointment could penetrate the dentine.

When the fox tried to open his mouth, however, his teeth were stuck together.

Oh my, Doctor De Soto said, excuse me, I forgot to tell you that you will not be able to open your mouth for a day or two in order for the ointment to really work. But not to worry, no toothaches ever again!

And while Doctor De Soto and his wife smiled at him, all the fox could say was, Frank oo berry mush, as he stumbled down the stairs, stunned at what had just happened.

And so, Huk concluded, Doctor De Soto and his wife had outfoxed the fox.

That's a great tale, Tuk said. But I have a question for you. The De Sotos chose to lie, right? Is that okay?

Well, said Huk, I guess it depends. Maybe lying is not the *right* thing to do, but it may be the *necessary* thing to do in some cases, like this one. They chose the necessary thing to do over the right thing to do.

I think this tale is about hard choices, Huk continued. The De Sotos had to decide, or choose, to let the fox in — twice — and then they had to make the choice to lie about the so-called ointment to prevent toothaches in order to protect their lives.

And look, Huk went on, they helped the fox out of his misery. They didn't have to do that. And they gave him a brand-new gold tooth. They didn't have to do that either.

Given what they were willing to do for him, they then had to do what they needed to do to save their own lives from a fox who was ready to eat them.

It was clear that the fox had no intention of sparing their little lives, Tuk said. He didn't even try to resist the urge to eat them after they had helped him out. They could have let him go on suffering with his bad tooth.

That's what I don't like, Tuk continued. I get it, he's a fox, but I think he's a mean fox because he doesn't even consider the fate of the De Sotos. And what's more important, lying about some ointment or saving your life from a mean fox?

Huk had to admit that saving your life was definitely more important.

Both Huk and Tuk were truly impressed with the De Sotos' courage. They must have been afraid to let the fox in and treat him the way they would any other patient. And so, they also took responsibility for lying to the fox in order to save their own lives.

Well, Huk mused, they saved their own lives, but if in fact Doctor De Soto was the only dentist in town, who would all the animals go to when they had dental problems if the fox had eaten the De Sotos? So, this fox is selfish, too, because he expects to be helped with *his* toothache but doesn't care that if he eats the De Sotos, the other animals have nobody to go to when they have tooth pain.

Well, Tuk concluded. They saved their own lives by keeping their eyes wide open when deciding how best to help this mean fox out of his misery and keep themselves safe at the same time. Those are the hardest decisions to make. Of course, it would have been easier to just decide not to help him or be foolish in thinking the fox would never harm them because they helped him. Making hard choices is really complicated.

You know, Huk said, come to think of it, when we had tails and were connected to the world and others around us, we were very careful about our decisions because we knew how they would affect others. When we lost our tails, we became less mindful and often made decisions that were bad for the world and others around us. It's as though we've been living with our eyes half closed, like the boy who never even considered the tree in his decisions and always wanted more from her.

And, said Tuk, continuing Huk's thought, since we didn't feel connected, we felt we had all these missing pieces and started looking for them. But these missing pieces never made us feel connected in the way we did when we had our tails. And ... in trying to find all these missing pieces, we started to take the world for granted.

Hmm ... Huk mused, when we feel connected to the world and others around us, we don't even think of ourselves as being incomplete and having missing pieces.

I like that, Tuk said, then added, To be connected, we have to keep our eyes wide open, like Sandy and Tico and the De Sotos. And then we can make good decisions too.

Huk started to laugh. I think philosophy, as an art, said Huk, is really the art of keeping our eyes wide open.

I think so too, Tuk agreed.

References

Lionni, Leo. *Tico and the Golden Wings*. New York: Dragonfly Books, 1964.

Lobel, Arnold. "Always" in *Grasshopper on the Road*. New York: Harper & Row Publishers, 1978.

———. "Alone," in *Days with Frog and Toad*. New York: HarperCollins Publishers, 1979.

Silverstein, Shel. *The Giving Tree*. New York: HarperCollins Publishers, 1964.

———. *The Missing Piece*. New York: HarperCollins Publishers, 1976.

Steig, William. *Doctor De Soto*. New York: Farrar, Straus and Giroux, 1982.

Acknowledgements

I would like to acknowledge the students and teachers at El Toyon Elementary School in San Diego, California. For three years, I conducted in-person classes in philosophy with students at El Toyon from the first, second and third grades. I would begin each class by reading a picture book, then I would ask the students to think about the questions that came up for them and to discuss these questions in small groups. Finally, students would write down their thoughts about the story and draw pictures. During those three years, I worked with teachers Yen Dang, Silvia Toledo, Patricia Carrillo, Pat Duran and Elizabeth McEvoy. I am thankful to these teachers for their dedication to doing philosophy with children and for encouraging the students to think for themselves. In the last two years, during COVID-19 lockdowns and restrictions, I continued working with Patricia Carrillo and Yen Dang, who would do read-alouds of the stories discussed by Huk and Tuk and ask the children to draw their thoughts and feelings about each story. I am thankful to both of them for continuing to explore these important questions with their students when I couldn't be in the classroom with them.

I want to thank the parents who gave permission to use their children's drawings as illustrations for the books. I am very grateful that we were able to continue the *Why We Are in Need of Tales* series in spite of all the additional pressure teachers had to cope with during the pandemic.

Once again, I am always grateful for the feedback from my friend and colleague Claartje van Sijl and, of course, from Mr. Lizzard.

Finally, thank you to Iguana Books, especially its publisher, Meghan Behse, and my editor, Holly Warren, who has been a delight to work with. If anyone gets what Huk and Tuk are about, it's Holly.

Maria daVenza Tillmanns

Maria teaches a "Philosophy with Children" program in underserved San Diego schools in partnership with the University of California, San Diego. In 1980, she attended Dr. Matthew Lipman's workshop on philosophy for children and later wrote her dissertation on philosophical counseling and teaching under the direction of Martin Buber scholar Dr. Maurice Friedman. She has publications in a number of international journals. For Maria, philosophy is an art form, and she enjoys painting with ideas. Philosophy has helped her navigate the world in all its complexity, including having a multicultural background and having been raised in the US as well as in the Netherlands. She came back to the US to study and moved across the Atlantic multiple times.